SUPERSCIENCE
INFOGRAPHICS

LIFE SCIENCE THROUGH INFOGRAPHICS

Nadia Higgins

graphics by Lisa Waananen

Lerner Publications Company
Minneapolis

To my father, who sees the beauty of science in all living things

Lerner Publications Company
A division of Lerner Publishing Group, Inc.
241 First Avenue North
Minneapolis, MN U.S.A. 55401

Website address: www.lernerbooks.com

Main text set in Univers LT Std 12/15.
Typeface provided by Adobe Systems.

Library of Congress Cataloging-in-Publication Data
Higgins, Nadia.
    Life science through infographics / by Nadia Higgins.
        p.   cm. — (Super science infographics)
    Includes index
    ISBN 978–1–4677–1288–0 (lib. bdg. : alk. paper)
    ISBN 978–1–4677–1787–8 (eBook)
    1. Life cycles (Biology)—Juvenile literature. 2. Evolution—
Juvenile literature. I. Title.
    QH501.H54   2014
    571.8—dc23   2013004839

Manufactured in the United States of America
1 – BP – 7/15/13

CONTENTS

LIFE-A-WHIRL

Do you have a future as a life scientist?
To find out, take this test.

When you walk down the sidewalk, do you stop to look at plants and bugs?

Do you enjoy pondering Big Questions, like "What is life?"

Do you like to geek out on amazing animal facts?

Have you and your friends ever pretended to be bacteria?

Did you answer yes to any of those questions?

CONGRATULATIONS!

You have what it takes to be a budding biologist—a scientist who studies living things. And, wow, there are lots of ways to do that! You can focus on animals (zoology), plants (botany), fungi (mycology), reptiles (herpetology), or insects (entomology). And that's just naming a few.

Is your head spinning yet? That happens to biologists sometimes. After all, LIFE is a pretty big topic. Biologists use graphs, charts, and other infographics to help sort through all the information. These graphics can make those big, mysterious ideas a bit clearer. Are you ready to join in the fun? Let's get started!

ORGANISMS RULE!

What does it take to be alive? You have to grow, and your species must be able to reproduce. You must also use some kind of energy. And you respond to what's around you, like heat and light. Finally, adapting to your environment is a major plus.

Organisms are creatures that meet these requirements. Scientists estimate that about 11.3 million species of organisms are on Earth. They fall into six main groups, called kingdoms.

BACTERIA

These microscopic, one-celled creatures are the simplest, oldest forms of life. They live everywhere, from the Arctic and the desert to your intestines.

ARCHAEA

These guys used to be in the bacteria group. It turns out their one-celled bodies work a lot differently than bacteria. So Archaea belong to their own group.

PROTISTS

These one-celled organisms are bigger and more complex than bacteria. Amoeba and mildew go here.

IT'S A BUG'S WORLD

Scientists estimate that about 6.8 million animal species live on Earth. Of these, 5 million are insects.

26% OTHER INVERTEBRATES

INSECTS 73%

— VERTEBRATES

Mammals....... 7%
Birds.............12%
Reptiles..........12%
Amphibians...19%
Fish...............50%

FUNGI

Mushrooms, yeast, lichen, and some bread molds are all types of fungi. Many fungi feast on dead things, turning them into soil.

PLANTS

Mosses, ferns, evergreens, and flowering plants—what do they have in common? Nearly all plants use the sun's energy to make food. It's called photosynthesis.

ANIMALS

Most animals are invertebrates, with no skeleton. Think insects, worms, sponges, jellyfish, clams, and starfish. Vertebrates, animals with skeletons, are less common. They include fish, reptiles, birds, amphibians, and mammals.

PARTY, EVOLUTION-STYLE

Imagine you're a hot-pink toad living in hot-pink surroundings. Lucky you! Your color hides you. So you don't get eaten, like your neon-blue neighbor does. You pass on pinkness to your kids. And they survive at higher rates. Then they pass on their color too. Eventually, your whole species could change.

That process is called natural selection. And it's one of the main forces behind evolution—the idea that living things change ever so slightly with each generation. Over billions of years, evolution has led to thousands of life-forms. Scientists divide the history of evolution into time periods. Each new period marks when conditions on Earth changed.

3,800 MILLION YEARS AGO (MYA) Bacteria form in ancient seas. All life—plants, fungi, and animals—will evolve from these first life-forms.

AROUND 1,000 MYA Complex life, such as algae, appears on the scene. Some early, soft-bodied animals may have formed too.

Animals are sporting hard body parts.

PRECAMBRIAN

Animal life takes off in the seas.

Jawless fish pave the way for vertebrates.

Mossy plants are the first organisms to move from water to land.

The first amphibians crawl out of the water.

The first true dinosaurs (and a few small mammals) roam the land.

Insects are gigantic.

Dinosaurs rule.

Birds have started evolving from dinosaurs.

65 MYA Dinosaurs go extinct.

Mammals get a lot bigger and more diverse.

Flowers and bees are having a heyday.

Sharks rule the seas.

QUATERNARY

4 MYA Early hominids, our ancestors, evolve in East Africa—finally!

2.5 MYA TO 30,000 Prehistoric humans are spreading around the planet on two feet.

200,000 YEARS AGO Hello, Homo sapiens! (That's us!)

CAMBRIAN

ORDOVICIAN

SILURIAN

DEVONIAN

CARBONIFEROUS

PERMIAN

TRIASSIC

JURASSIC

CRETACEOUS

TERTIARY

ROCK STARS

Scientists know a lot about how animals evolved. They also know about when it happened. But *how* do they know? That's a good (and very scientific) question! The answer comes down to fossils. Scientists study these ancient remains of plants and animals like clues. Fossils help scientists piece together the story of life.

It's hard to become a fossil. Just a tiny number of organisms manage to do it. Take a look at some ways to fossil fame.

BODY FOSSILS

WHAT: Preserved bones, shells, feathers, wood, seeds, leaves, pollen, and microbes.

WHY WE LOVE 'EM: Two words—dinosaur bones.

HOW THEY HELP: They are often discovered in layers of rock. The layers are organized by oldest at the bottom to newest on top. This is one major way scientists piece together the story of evolution.

TRACE FOSSILS

WHAT: Nests, burrows, eggs, teeth marks, footprints, poop, and other signs of ancient animal activity.

WHY WE LOVE 'EM: Each of these rare finds gives us new info about ancient life.

HOW THEY HELP: They tell how animals traveled, found food, cared for their young, and so much more.

LIVING FOSSILS

WHAT: Okay, these aren't actually fossils. But these living species have changed very little over millions of years. Horseshoe crabs and ginkgo trees are good examples.

WHY WE LOVE 'EM: These throwbacks are like fossils in motion. So freaky!

HOW THEY HELP: Scientists compare them to their ancient relatives. Then they can fill in gaps in fossil history.

CHEMICAL FOSSILS

WHAT: Chemicals found in ancient rocks. These chemicals resulted from living things changing the chemicals of the rock.

WHY WE LOVE 'EM: They are the most ancient fossils out there.

HOW THEY HELP: They reveal the earliest signs of life.

OUR WORLD'S WORLDS

In nature, everything works together—the climate, the land, and all living things. Together, they create a biome, a region on Earth where specific groups of species live.

OCEANS

Oceans cover more than two-thirds of our planet. They also get the prize for having the weirdest creatures. Colorful sponges, glowing fish, and seaweed all live here.

CORAL REEFS

These colorful reefs are the skeletons of creatures called coral. They grow in warm, shallow waters. And they provide homes for some of the planet's most varied and beautiful creatures.

POLAR REGIONS

These places aren't just incredibly cold. They're also dry. Polar regions don't host a lot of species. But the ones they have often come in huge numbers.

TROPICAL FORESTS

It's mostly warm, humid, and green along the equator. This biome gets the prize for most species. Think tree frogs, spider monkeys, boa constrictors, orangutans, and parrots (and lots and lots of insects).

CONIFEROUS FORESTS

Tall, hardy evergreens fill these northern forests. They are home to prowling bears and howling wolves.

TEMPERATE FORESTS

Seasons rule in this biome. Trees lose their leaves in fall and get new ones in spring. Animals scurry below, and owls fly overhead. Plenty of slugs, snails, and turtles deserve attention too.

DESERTS

Deserts make up the largest land biome. They cover about one-third of our planet's land. Organisms living here survive with little water.

GRASSLANDS

These enormous stretches of grasses are marked by few trees. Grazing animals, such as zebras, live here. So do their predators, such as lions, hawks, and hyenas.

MOUNTAINS

The higher you go, the colder, wetter, and windier it gets. The air has less oxygen too. Hardy bighorn sheep and golden eagles live here. So do low-lying mosses and shrubs.

13

THANK YOU, DNA

Nearly all cells contain DNA in one way or another. This super-important molecule is the boss of every living thing—including you. Your DNA was passed down to you from both your parents. Just like their DNA was passed down from their parents. It carries the instructions that made you *you.* In many ways, it decides who you are, how you will grow, and what you look like.

Most DNA molecules are shaped like a twisted ladder. Each DNA rung contains a pair of DNA units, called bases. The bases are like puzzle pieces. Only four different combos "fit" together: A-T, T-A, C-G, or G-C. But each DNA molecule has billions of rungs. The order and number of rungs is what matters. It's a kind of code. Your DNA code determines if you are a human, an apple, or an aardvark.

Your DNA code is totally your own. The closer you're related to someone, the more your DNA matches up. Identical twins have almost perfectly matching DNA.

On average, the difference between one human's DNA code and another human's is just 0.1 percent.

DNA BASES

The bases have fancy chemical names. But even scientists use just the first letter.

A   T   C   G

Humans share genes with all living things. Chimpanzees and bonobos are our closest relatives. We share 98.8 percent of our genetic code with these furry relatives.

Small sections of DNA called genes can determine specific traits, such as curly hair, freckles, or even how far back your thumb bends. Many genes just keep our bodies running! Human DNA contains around 20,000 genes.

CHROMOSOME CLOSE-UP

A DNA molecule is tightly packaged inside a chromosome.

Human chromosomes come in pairs.

We have 23 pairs in every cell nucleus, except our reproduction cells. Those have only 23 chromosomes total.

15

LET'S GET MICROSCOPIC

All it takes is one cell to be an organism. Just ask bacteria. But what is a cell, exactly? It's the simplest unit of life. Imagine if your body were made of veeeery small Lego bricks. A cell would be just one of those bricks.

Different cells have different jobs. Your body has trillions of cells. But all cells have this in common: they're crazy busy. They're like little factories keeping you alive. Take the skin cell. Every year, about 9 pounds (4 kilograms) of dead skin cells flake off your body. And yet . . . you're even bigger. Like most cells, skin cells can reproduce. How does it work? Check it out.

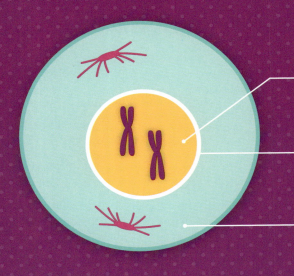

GETTING READY

NUCLEUS: This is the cell's control center. It contains chromosomes—packets of DNA. The DNA gets copied as the cell prepares to split.

NUCLEAR MEMBRANE: This "skin" decides what comes in and what goes out. It keeps everything in place.

CYTOPLASM: This is where all other important organelles in a cell are located.

MICROSCOPIC OUTLAWS

Viruses are a kind of germ. They cause everything from colds to warts to rabies. Like living cells, they carry DNA. But they can't reproduce like living things. So viruses are cell hijackers. They inject their DNA into a living cell of an organism (like you). That turns the cell into the virus's slave. The virus uses the cell to make copies of itself. Those new viruses break out of the slave cell. Then they move on to their next cell victims.

T4 BACTERIOPHAGE

Virus injects DNA into the cell.

LIVING CELL

STREEEEETCH!

1. The membrane around the nucleus dissolves.

2. The chromosomes line up in the center of the cell. Then one copy of each chromosome is pulled to each side.

3. The cell narrows in the middle and splits.

IT'S TWINS!

1. New membranes form after the cell has divided in half.

2. The two cells have identical copies of DNA and are ready to begin the process again.

17

AMAZING BODS

Here's another way to think about living things: they are survival machines. Their bodies have evolved to face the challenges of their surroundings. Their physical features help organisms find food, communicate, find mates, and more.

CHEETAH

This fierce predator is the fastest animal on four legs. It reaches speeds of 64 mph (104 kph).

Eyes face forward. That lets the cheetah judge how far it needs to run to chase its prey.

Flexible backbone arches up and down to lengthen each stride.

Whiskers pick up vibrations in the air.

Bulky muscle is high on thigh, so lighter bottom leg swings effortlessly.

Claws retract (pull in) for silent, sneaky footsteps.

Sharp teeth are shaped for stabbing as well as slicing.

AMAZON WATER LILY

Rimmed edges make sure other leaves don't grow over it.

1 FOOT (0.3 METERS)

Air-filled tubes inside keep the leaf afloat.

10 FEET (3 METERS)

Giant leaf blocks light below it, so no other competing plants can grow.

Sharp spines underneath keep fish from nibbling.

WANDERING ALBATROSS

This bird spends most of its time flying over the ocean. Incredibly long wings are good for gliding. It can soar for hours without a single flap.

11 FEET (3.5 METERS)

Hooked tip with sharp edges grips slippery ocean prey.

Spits up smelly stomach oil to turn off predators. Also makes nutritious food for its young.

Skull bones filled with air pockets so giant head is not too heavy.

4 FEET (1.2 METERS)

Huge ears have a network of blood vessels inside. Elephant flaps ears to release extra body heat into the air.

AFRICAN ELEPHANT

Trunk is nimble enough to pluck blades of grass.

Tough skin, up to 2 inches (5 cm) thick, protects like a wrinkled suit of armor.

GIANT STICK INSECT

This creature can barely move or fly. So how does it keep away predators? It tricks them by looking like a stick.

Hook-like feet keep it from falling off its branch.

PIDDOCK

Shell edge can dig out a burrow in wood or rock.

Water pumps inside the shell through a tube. Sticky mucus traps bits of food in the water. Tiny hairs push food to the mouth.

ELECTRIC EEL

Body makes deadly jolts of electricity that kill prey.

THE CIRCLE OF LIFE

All living things grow, and they all reproduce. Then a new generation repeats the process. That's the life cycle for you. Of course, species' life cycles happen in dazzlingly different ways. Here's how one species, the convergent lady beetle, does it.

2 TO 5 DAYS LATER

1 The female lays clusters of fertilized eggs. She looks for a protected place with plenty of aphid insects. That way, her larvae will have plenty to eat once they hatch.

THE CYCLE BEGINS AGAIN

4 "I can fly!" The adult ladybug starts looking for a mate. The male fertilizes her eggs. And the life cycle starts all over again.

2 Larvae look like tiny alligators. They eat aphids like crazy. They grow fast, shedding their skin three times.

20 TO 30 DAYS LATER

3 The chubby larva attaches itself to the underside of a leaf. Then it turns into a pupa. A complete makeover is under way.

3 TO 12 DAYS LATER

EAT AND BE EATEN

A species of insect is dying off in a lake by your home. So what, right? Wait! What about the fish that eat that insect . . . and the birds that eat those fish? Even the most annoying insect is part of a food web. Every living thing plays a role in the overall balance of life. A food chain shows what living things are eaten by others. As they feast on one another, energy and nutrients are passed along.

A FOOD CHAIN is part of a food web. It all starts with energy from the sun. Take a look at one common type of food chain.

Plants turn sunlight into food through photosynthesis.

1. PRODUCERS
All plants belong here. They store energy from the sun. They form the foundation of most food chains.

2. PRIMARY CONSUMER
These animals eat plants. Lots of insects and birds belong here. So do many rodents, like mice and rabbits. They store energy from plants in their cells.

3. SECONDARY CONSUMER
Next up, animals that eat plant-eating animals. Think of your cat eating a mouse.

CITY FOOD WEB

Of course, animals don't eat just one kind of food. And they don't fit neatly into food-chain categories. Just think of omnivores, animals that eat both meat and plants. Food chains link up into a tangle of food webs. Here's what a food web in your neighborhood might look like.

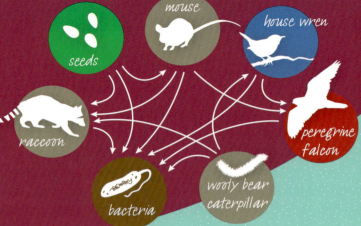

Yellow arrows show the flow of **ENERGY** from one life-form to the next. With each arrow, energy is lost.

Pink arrows show how **NUTRIENTS** are recycled.

4. TERTIARY CONSUMER

These carnivores eat other meat eaters, as well as plant-eating animals. These are the food chain's top dogs. They have no natural predators. Think of a wolf that tries to eat your cat.

5. SCAVENGERS AND DECOMPOSERS

Scavengers are animals that eat dead plants and animals. (After that wolf has died, a vulture might eat the wolf's remains.) Decomposers are creepy-crawlies like maggots, fungi, and bacteria that feast on dead things and poop. Decomposers turn nature's leftovers into rich soil that helps plants grow.

The soil helps plants grow. In this way, nutrients passed along the food chain are recycled.

THE WOW-O-METER OF LIFE

Let's face it. Life is freaky. Need proof? Look no further.

LEAPIN' FLEAS!

A cat flea can leap 170 times the length of its body!

SAY AHHHHHHHHHHH

A chameleon's tongue is as long as its body.

YOU DON'T SAY!

NO WAY!

WALK MUCH?

The millipede species *Llacme plenipes* has 750 legs!

DON'T CALL ME

The blue whale isn't just the largest animal. It's the loudest. In fact, its call is louder than a jet engine.

SUDDENLY, I FEEL ITCHY

You are outnumbered by insects by 2 billion to 1.

STICK WITH ROSES

The corpse flower blooms every four to six years for one day. Good thing! The flower smells exactly like rotting flesh.

THAT EXPLAINS A LOT!

You have about 40,000 species of bacteria living in your gut.

GET A LOAD OF THIS!

Imagine you could weigh all the ants in the world. Together, they'd weigh more than all Earth's mammals combined.

WILD!

I THINK MY HEAD JUST EXPLODED!

NEVER SAY DIE

One spruce tree in Sweden is more than 9,500 years old. That means it sprouted during the Ice Age!

THE BAD NEWS

It's a sad but true fact of nature: species go extinct. In fact, 99 percent of species that ever lived on Earth have died off. In the past, though, volcanoes, asteroids, and other natural events caused extinction. Right this minute, the planet is undergoing the highest rates of extinction ever. Today, human activity is the driving force. The things we do, like growing food or building homes, have always affected nature. As our population has skyrocketed, those activities are causing big problems.

THE RED LIST

The International Union for Conservation of Nature (IUCN) works to protect endangered species. Its Red List of Threatened Species is the world's best record of endangered plants and animals. The IUCN is still gathering complete info on insects and other major categories. But their research paints a vivid picture.

PERCENTAGE OF SPECIES THAT ARE THREATENED

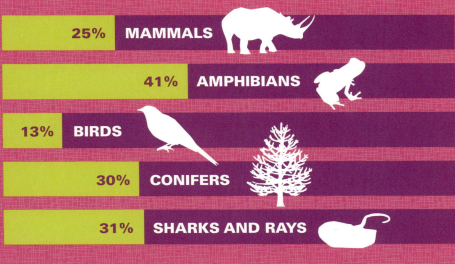

25% MAMMALS

41% AMPHIBIANS

13% BIRDS

30% CONIFERS

31% SHARKS AND RAYS

HABITAT DESTRUCTION
Species are losing places to hunt, raise their young, and find food.

CAUSES: growing cities, farms, and mining

AIR AND WATER POLLUTION
Pollution is harming habitats and food sources.

CAUSES: factories, crop pesticides and herbicides

OVERFISHING AND ILLEGAL HUNTING
Fish and endangered species are being lost.

CAUSES: high global demand for fish, sale of wild animals as pets, for their body parts, and for meat

INTRUDER SPECIES
Nonnative animals and plants crowd out local species.

CAUSES: plants and animals transported to places they don't belong, poor laws that are difficult to enforce

CLIMATE CHANGE
Global changes in climate are disrupting life cycles, food webs, and more.

CAUSES: greenhouse gases (carbon dioxide) from cars, power plants, and other industries

10 WAYS TO LIVE GREEN

"Think globally. Act locally." It's not just a cheesy bumper sticker. It means that you can take small actions—right now—that will help polar bears in the Arctic. Check out these ten ideas for living in harmony with your planet.

1. DO THE THREE R'S

And in the right order: reduce, reuse, recycle. What's one of the best things you can do for Earth? Don't buy stuff you don't need—like another plastic thingy that will spend 500 years in a landfill.

2. VOTE WITH YOUR DOLLARS

Every time you spend a dollar, you're telling a business you like it. So vote for businesses that show they care about Earth!

3. BE CHOOSY ABOUT WHAT YOU EAT

Raising farm animals is a lot harder on Earth than growing veggies. How about skipping meat one day a week? Another biggie—don't waste food.

4. MAKE CARS ENDANGERED

Pollution from cars is a huge cause of climate change. Cut back by walking or biking when you can.

5. DON'T BE A WATER HOG

The water from your tap has to be treated so it's safe to drink. That's hard on the environment. One of the best ways to save water is by doing less laundry. Put your half-worn clothes on a hook, and wear them again a few days later.

6. GROW LOCAL

Grow native plants. These are plants that naturally belong in your biome. They'll thrive in your garden. So will the local birds and bugs that feed on them.

7. COMPOST

Your kitchen scraps and yard waste will make THE best soil for your native plant garden. Plus, you'll be helping to keep landfills under control.

8. TAKE A HIKE

Nature reserves provide habitats for all kinds of plants and animals. Support them with a visit—and bring your friends too.

9. MAKE YOUR PARENTS CRY

Make a difference on your next birthday. Ask Mom and Dad for a membership to an organization that protects wildlife. Or make a donation in your parents' names on their birthdays.

10. SPEAK UP

Is your school practicing the three Rs? What about your community center or place of worship? Are your elected officials doing all they can to make Earth-friendly laws? No? Then say something! But be smart. Present solid facts, and offer solutions when you can.

Glossary

BIOME: a region on Earth where specific groups of species live. Oceans, tropical forests, and mountains are examples of biomes.

CELL: a basic unit of all living things. All cells contain DNA.

CHROMOSOME: a DNA "package" inside a cell. In humans, chromosomes come in threadlike pairs.

CLIMATE CHANGE: also known as global warming, the overall warming of Earth's atmosphere. Climate change could be a major contributor to species loss.

DNA: short for **d**eoxyribo**n**ucleic **a**cid, this chemical substance stores the code that controls cells and determines genetic traits.

EVOLUTION: the scientific theory that all species developed from the simplest life-forms. Over millions of years, animals and plants became more complex and diverse.

EXTINCT: died out. An extinct species no longer exists on the planet.

FERTILIZE: to make an egg able to grow. Eggs are female cells that are fertilized by male cells.

GENE: a section of DNA that determines a specific trait, such as eye color. Human DNA has about 20,000 genes.

LARVA: a baby insect that often looks like a worm. A larva will change completely as it grows.

MOLECULE: a basic unit of matter. A molecule is made of two or more atoms.

ORGANISM: a living thing. You, your pets, potted plants, and bacteria are all organisms.

PHOTOSYNTHESIS: a chemical process in which green plants use sunlight, water, and carbon dioxide to make food. Photosynthesis is why plants die if they don't get the right amount of sunlight.

POLLEN: a yellow "dust" inside flowers that is used to fertilize a plant's egg and turn it into a seed. Bees spread dusty pollen from flower to flower, helping plants make seeds.

PUPA: an insect stage of life, when a larva turns into an adult. A pupa is often inside a cocoon.

SPECIES: a kind of organism. Members of a species can mate and create offspring.

Animal Planet: *Weird, True & Freaky*
http://animal.discovery.com/tv
-shows/weird-true-and-freaky
Catch up on all the videos you missed, including "Top 5 Grossest Animal Jobs," "Bull Shark Attack," and "World's First Bionic Cat."

Brown, Jordan D. *Micro Mania: A Really Close-Up Look at Bacteria, Bedbugs, & the Zillions of Other Gross Little Creatures That Live In, On, & All Around You.* Watertown, MA: Imagine, 2011.
Guaranteed to make you feel itchy, this fun book will make you squeal at least once.

Discover the Forest
http://www.discovertheforest.org
This awesome site helps you find woods nearby and gives tips for making the most of your outdoor adventure.

"Everything Has a Life Cycle"
http://www.youtube.com
/watch?v=O3uLKoortQk
Brought to you by Bill Nye the Science Guy, this fun parody of a '70s hit song is guaranteed to keep you singing about life cycles all day.

Exploratorium: Living Things
http://www.exploratorium.edu
/explore/living_things
From mutant fruit flies to zebra fish to Neanderthal bones . . . this off-the-wall site offers activities, articles, and videos on the coolest topics out there.

Fact Monster: Biology
http://www.factmonster.com
/science/biology
This site offers solid info that's easy to find—a great first stop for reports.

Hauth, Katherine B. *What's for Dinner? Quirky, Squirmy Poems from the Animal World.* Watertown, MA: Charlesbridge, 2011.
Who doesn't love funny biology poems with wacky cartoon illustrations?

National Geographic Kids: Animals & Pets
http://kids.nationalgeographic.com
/kids/animals
Cool videos, games, articles—and a chance to watch polar bears live!

Pringle, Laurence. *Billions of Years, Amazing Changes: The Story of Evolution.* Honesdale, PA: Boyds Mills, 2011.
Enjoy a really clear, step-by-step explanation of evolution, with lots of examples to share with your friends.

Wojahn, Rebecca Hogue, and Donald Wojahn. *A Coral Reef Food Chain: A Who-Eats-What Adventure in the Caribbean Sea.* Minneapolis: Lerner Publications, 2010.
As if food chains weren't exciting enough, you get to pick you own adventure in this colorful, info-packed book.